PSALMS OF MY SOUL

MRS. R. EZHILARASI

DEDICATION

This book is dedicated

- To my soulmate Mr. R. Logabiraman,
- To my parents for always loving and supporting me,
- To all my teachers who brightened my life.

Contents

Contents

Contents

Contents

Contents

Disclaimer

This cute compilation of 100 poems contain write ups on various topics.

The write ups published are the author's original content.

The author guarantees that the content is plagiarism free.

Preface

PREFACE

"Poetry has its origin in emotions
Recollected in tranquility."
William wordsworth

Poetry is the rhythmical creation of emotions in words. It takes its origin from mind and soul. It is the art of writing and correlating beauty, emotions with truth. Filling the paper with words from own experience of joy and sorrow with cute imagination is Poetry.

A Poet is a person who is passionately in love with nature and language. Poets always utter good and wise things. The author of the book as a language lover, started discovering her writing in Creative Writers and Versatile Writers Group, a group of English teachers and poetry lovers. As a result, here comes short and sweet Poems "Psalms of my soul" a collection of hundred poems to reach your hands like a peaceful dove. I assure all that this book will be thought provoking and also a great feast for poetry lovers.

Acknowledgements

First and foremost, I thank God for his blessings showered on me in completing this book successfully.

I would like to express my heartfelt thanks to Mrs. D. Brinda, Admin of Creative Writers Whatsapp group for her motivation and guidance.

I owe my gratitude from the depth of my heart to my beloved Teachers Mr. T. Arulappan, Principal, Sarvodhaya Nursery & Primary school, Manavur, Thiruvellore Dt. and Mrs. A. Sumathy, Vice Principal, for the wonderful foreword and blessings.

I would like to express my sincere gratitude to Mrs. D. Brinda, Graduate Teacher (English), GHS, Melapattampakkam, Cuddalore Dt., Mr. S.K. Kumaran, Graduate Teacher (English), TMKV GBHSS, Kangeyanallur, Vellore Dt., Mrs. A. Princilin Joan, Graduate Teacher (English), P.U.M.S, Puliyamangalam, Ranipet Dt. for contributing their fantastic foreword for this book.

My sincere thanks to Mrs. S. Suja Devi, Headmistress, GGHSS, Arakkonam and Mr. A. Siva, Asst. Headmaster, GGHSS, Arakkonam, Dr. A. Mathini, Asst.Prof, SCSVMV University, Enathur Kancheepuram for their kindness and support.

My hearty thanks to Mrs. S. Sumathi, Graduate Teacher (English), Sri KGS HSS, Aduthurai, Thanjavur dt., for the timely help and technical support in publishing this book.

I am grateful to my friend Mrs. B.Deepa, Graduate Teacher (English), GGHSS, Arakkonam who always encourage me and helps me to develop my ideas.

I would like to acknowledge with gratitude for the support and love of my family members, especially my son L.E. Manorajapriyan and my daughter

L.E Prithika for the good times in my life.

Finally, I offer my regards and blessings to all those who supported me in any respect for the publication of this book.

Foreword

Mrs. D. BRINDA, M.A., M.Phill., B.Ed.,PGDELT.
ENGLISH GRADUATE TEACHER
GOVT HIGH SCHOOL, MELPATTAMPAKKAM,
CUDDALORE, TAMILNADU.

I am happy to script a few words for this book **Psalms of my soul**. This book contains 100 poems on various topics of life. The poet Mrs. R. Ezhilarasi is regular, sincere, and a hardworking teacher. She is regular in posting poems in Creative Writers group. Her words and thoughts are awesome. She has expressed in a nice way. If I am not wrong this author has started her poetic journey in this Creative Writers group in the year 2020, but she has a lot of feelings lying deep in her heart. it is that time she joined

Creative Writers' group and started to pen her feelings with enthusiasm.

She takes part not only in writing verses but also in all the activities of Creative Writers. She takes part in online poetry competition, anthology and other activities. She is a good reviewer who reviews fellow poets. Her poems have got amazing reviews from co- poets.

She starts the book with the topic 'Flower'. It takes the readers to a beautiful journey. The rhythmic movement of her verses move like waves. Plenty of images are used to decorate the verses. They really add beauty, charm and grace to all the verses. The rhyming words used are simply amazing. It makes the readers read again and again. Every minute things are given prominent importance like 'The story of footwear', Many historical importance is also brought out then and there like Mahabalipuram. The poem 'Jackfruit' really brings water in our tongue, juicy and sweet fruit.

Smile is very important to all the human. This is brought out in the poem rightly in 'Smile'. It is a powerful weapon which destroys anger and enmity. Heavy burden changes to a lovely Garden. This poem is a class one.

"Peace begins with smile.

Smile can change the world for a while."

For all the writers the magic wand is only their own pen. They fight for the right of human. Of course, it is non-violent. 'Twinkling stars' is knitted so well with the beautiful rhyming words. This is the plus point in her book. The poet brings history in some of her poems.

Some of her poems really remind of our good old days. Reminiscence of the past. Poem 'Grandmother' brings the exact picture of many grandmothers. Some proverbs like 'Health is wealth' tells the deep truth. We understand the real value of health only when we are unwell. To be in good health we need to do a lot of practical things. Everything is clearly explained inch by inch. The poem everyone must adhere without a second thought.

Many of us have some doubt of real beauty. It is not in face or skin. The outward skin beauty is only skin deep. Real beauty lies in the beautiful heart which is so nice. To tell about the titles or the topics all simply captivating making us read it without skipping any poem. Forget and forgive is the strongest and first to forget is the happiest. How nicely it is portrayed. In some of her poems I smell John Keats, Byron, William Wordsworth. In the poem nature speaks, really nature speaks. Only thing is that we have to lend our ears to listen and enjoy the nature. To avoid pollution, we have to find a solution. Positive words are penned here. I will not give up. Some poems are simple but they have in-depth meaning like Mother, Friendship etc. "One Way Ticket To Moon" really took me to the space. Though it is imagination, it was nice to imagine. Dance, love, hate are clearly expressed with expression. Some poems are women related poems. They are given due importance. I loved the poem 'I heard a bird' and 'Like a fish hook', we have to be very careful in some situation. Who is richer speaks the reality of life. Many philosophical poems are there to give thought provoking ideas like Time management, Be innocent as a child to be Richer, When I close my eyes tells to confess wrong deeds and mistakes. She is determined not to tell mistakes and to believe gossips, not to be jealous on others. some heart touching poems have taken place in this book. They evoke tears in our eyes while reading. The day you left me expresses the sorrow of her grandmother's demise. This experience everyone might have come across. The poem dear Gopi ji, Letter to the dear departed soul, an Elegy to the Ki Ra are amazing. I salute poem gives honour to all the army members who guard and secure us from enemies. Their Unity is to be saluted. They are the guardian angels. They are really vigilant in the borders, ready to face any danger. The ultimate is she has given the same respect to the farmers ,doctors and other profession who play the major role in the society. Father's love is definitely higher than anyone. This is portrayed in her poem.

Writing has helped a lot. This is expressed in 'Writing helped me' in and 'Happy Birthday to you Creative Writers' they're simply amazing. I have only touched a few here. I have gone through all the poems line by line word by word between the lines and cherished thoroughly. Now I give the chance to all the readers to go through the poems patiently and enlighten yourself and get aesthetic pleasure.

Wish this book to reach many hands.

Mrs. D. Brinda

Foreword

Mr. T.Arullappan M.A.,M.A.,B.Ed.,Principal, Sarvodhaya Nursery & Primary School, Manavur, Thiruthani T.K., Thiruvellore District.

I am proud and happy to review the poems "Psalms of My Soul" of Mrs. R. Ezhilarasi. As I know her from her child hood, she is curious in reading and expressing her visions. She always thinks differently. I read all her 100 poems several times. It's very interesting to read and learn. I wonder how she could think like this! Good execution and expression of various thinking.

About "Psalms of My Soul" :

• All the poems are cute and meaningful.

Used most of the noble words in the Dictionary.

The poems touched all the stages of a human such as Child hood, Peer groups, Father, Mother, Grand mother and so on.

• Enlightened the Friendship, Love, Care and money.
• Gives future vision in the year 2050, past glory and present status.
• The words used in are simple and apt.
• The titles of poems tempt us to read.
• "Father is more than a hundred school masters". What a great philosophy!
• The author some where seems to be a child, some where a matured person, some where a thinker and a writer and some where a philosopher.
• All the poems are short and sweet.
• Each time we read, we get a new meaning.
• Night time beauty is explained sweetly in "Twinkling Stars"
• The poem "Grand Mother" is heart touching.
• "Where there is truth, there is God", what a definition!
• "Money is important but" - gives clear idea about money.
• "Education" proves its eminence and importance.
• Soldiers, Farmers, Doctors, Writers are saluted.

Do you want to know the answers to the following questions :

1. When does grief disappear?

2.Which is the powerful Weapon?

3. What is real Beauty?

4. What is Joy?

5. Who is a true companion?

6. What are the important things a person need?

7. Why do some behave rude?

8. What to do to have a better memory?

9. What determines our Present and Future?

10. Why should we "Learn to say No?"

If you go through the poems, you will get it.

Corona Virus gave damage to mankind and shuttered all their jobs but gave her a good time to write these Poems **"Psalms of My Soul"**. Writing **100 Poems** in **Various Titles** is not an easy thing. It's a great job and a useful treasure to the book lovers. My great wishes to her to bring more books like this. Keep it up.

Vazgha Valamudan.

By

Mr. T.Arullappan M.A.,M.A.,B.Ed.,

Foreword

Mrs. Y. PRINCILIN JOAN,English Graduate Teacher, P.U.M.

School,Puliyamangalam,Arakkonam.

I feel much delighted to write a foreword to Mrs. R. Ezhilarasi's book ' Psalms of My Soul'. She is an accomplished poet with abundant ideas. All her poems in the book are embedded with realistic touches and sparkles of insight. Her thoughts are unique that reflect her gleaming knowledge all over her work. The poem ' Smile' insists on re-examining the reason for well-being. And it rejuvenates the minds of readers as well. The poem ' Real beauty' celebrates the glory of the grandeur in every heart. It emphasizes mercy, charity, empathy, and sympathy in a unique manner. 'When nature speaks' is a poem of all time. It portrays the indomitable features of nature and induces the importance of preserving it. The poem' I salute' is a remarkable tribute to Soldiers, Farmers, and Doctors. 'Independent, yet in chains' is a well-knitted poem adorned with an impressive perspective. I am confident 'Psalms of My Soul' can reach the core of every heart and entertain all literary lovers. The psalms can soothe the souls and sow the fertile seeds of whatever the poet wants to plant there. I wish wholeheartedly for all her future endeavors. My best wishes for an amazing poetic journey ahead.

By

Mrs. **Y. PRINCILIN JOAN**

Foreword

Mr. S.K. KUMARAN

M.A (Eng), M.A.(Eco), M.sc (Psy) B.Ed., CELT Graduate Teacher

TMKV GBHSS, Kangeyanallur, Vellore.

I feel immense pleasure in giving the foreword for this book titled, "Psalms of My Soul" which was penned by Mrs. R. Ezhilarasi. Being the admin of "Versatile Writers "Whatsapp forum, I have cherished and relished the rhythmic verses of Mrs. R. Ezhilarasi. She is an inspirational teacher, fabulous facilitator and a soulful singer. She is cheerful, harmonious and exhibits a dazzling demeanor. Besides teaching, she has an elegant skill in knitting wonderful words. This book speaks about her relentless and scintillating soul.

The poetess has touched all the essential genres of the poetry and proved her efficacy through her manifold thoughts. She has a wide variety of poems in her "Psalms of My Soul". The poems like "Indian Culture", "Life is a game, play it" "You came into my life, like.." entice the readership and emanates frabjous thoughts. For instance in her poem "I don't allow myself to", she alluringly explains her self confidence, grit, and positive attitude. In the poem "An Empty Nest" The nesting skill of the bird was bestowed bewitchingly. In her poem "Forgiveness, thy name is Woman" reveals her revolutionary thoughts and throw light upon the imprecated injustice upon the women folk. The poem titled "Letter to the departed Soul" would stand as a testimony for her love and respect towards her Father-in-law whom she adorned a lot.

The famous writer Edgar Alan Poe says that, "Poetry is the rhythmical creation of beauty in words". These words suit to Mrs. R. Ezhilarasi, as her poems are enriched with rhyme, rhythm and imageries. For instance, in her poem. "The best in me", she cited as follows, "I never cheat a person who trust in me" the above lines, divulge her perspicacity and adroitness. She is very much specialized in creating rhythmic verses in the poems. I appreciate her diligence in publishing this book and I also wish her to be successful in all her future endeavors.

By

Mr. S.K. KUMARAN

1. FLOWERS

Blossoms are the gift of nature,

It reflects the beauty of God's creature

Gorgeous wedding garland makes bride and groom cheer,

Decorative wreath for deity, to wipe our tears.

Alluring bouquet to welcome great men and women,

Eye-catching parks and gardens are for recreation.

Awesome fragrance fills everyone with satisfaction.

On auspicious days it gives us gratification.

Be soft and spread fragrance like a rose,

Be gentle and enchant others as a jasmíne.

Be pure and divine like a lotus,

Be confident and enjoy life as a lily,

Don't blame, Bloom where you've been planted,

Learn from the flower to always give nectar.

2. THE STORY OF A FOOTWEAR

Footwear protects our feet
From all the encountering objects that hurt,
For an athlete sports shoes is a great support
To win many more medals with some effort.
Once I went on an school excursion to Mahabalipuram
Along with my friends, astonished to see the royal monuments,
Rock cut monuments in the temple shows the architect beauty of Pallavas
Shore temple, Cave temple and Rathas show their economic status.
When I was closer to the single stone elephant carving
My foot wear straps were torn unexpectedly,
As it was a hot noon, my feet couldn't bear the scorching sun
Believe it or not, I ran like an athlete to the comfort zone.

3. JACKFRUIT

Children are engaged with funny talk,
Teacher entered the classroom with a chalk.
She taught fruits and vegetables are nature's treat,
Jack fruit with a special aroma is so sweet.
It's the biggest tree borne fruit,
Yellow fruit bulbs are juicy and sweet.
Used to prepare custard, chips and cakes,
Mouth-watering fruit that everyone likes.
Flesh and seeds are high in nutrition,
Starch and fibers are good for digestion.
Seeds are compared to Brazil nuts,
Trees provide us with timber and latex.
Avoid junk foods and quit
Eat healthy fruit like 'Jack' and stay fit.

4. TRIBUTE TO PADMASHRI Dr. VIVEKANANDAN

Great men are always filled with fun,

Legendary person, who brightened all lives as the sun.

Through his dialogues and evergreen comedies,

Dreamt to build a nation free of pollution

So, he planted 33.3 lakh trees with gratification.

A very humble, spiritual and humorous person,

He was longing to create a society free of superstition.

"Thousands of spare parts are in the lorry

Why you people trust in a lemon makes me feel sorry".

It shows that his efforts and creations are meant for recreation.

Due to massive attack you passed away,

May your soul rest in peace, We all pray.

5. SMILE

Smile is a powerful weapon
It destroys the anger and enmity.
It is the gateway of humanity
Smile makes your heavy burden as a lovely garden.
Smile is a blessing to every human being
It's a free therapy for good health.
Charming smile of a baby brings heaven on earth
Smile! Be a reason for someone's well-being.
Smile could move tearing tension
It's the only remedy for many confusion
Life is like a mirror
Smile, you can wipe away all errors.
Smile is the best make-up any girl can wear
It reflects the sense of care
Peace begins with Smile
Smile, you can change the world awhile.

6. MY MAGIC WAND

My magical wand is pen
A mighty weapon for anyone,
Who fights for the rights of human
Pride to have one to fulfill my ambition.
A non-violent tool
Helps to express my thoughts so cool.
Created by human to destroy inhuman,
Trust, it transforms 'painful thorns' to 'Joyful crowns.'

7. TWINKLING STARS

The sun sets in the west
Sparrows and cuckoos fly to their nest,
Crescent like moon appears at first
Bright little stars decorate the sky like fest.
Children count the uncountable stars with interest
Sometimes they couldn't find one because of mist.
Many people wish to be a 'star' as the best,
It's time for many creatures to take a rest.
Once three wise men came from the east
Guided by the 'Twinkling star' reached so fast
Paid homage to child Jesus and felt like feast
Later, Jesus grew up and became a great priest.

8. GRANDMOTHER

Granny granny, tell me a story
Moral story to attain greater glory.
Your care makes me feel comfort
Succor for the family is a great support.
Granny granny, comb my hair,
Guide me to look so neat and fair.
Teach me how to give respect
Bless me to grow up so perfect.
Granny granny, share our family history
An inspiration to me to achieve many victory,
You encourage my intellectual growth
I'll follow your footsteps, It's my oath.

9. RAINBOW OF FEELINGS

Affection and care of a mother,
Love and support of a father,
Who hold us like an anchor,
Timely guidance of a teacher,
Immediate treatment given by a doctor,
Makes us happy like a colorful rainbow.
Sharing our joys and sorrows with friends,
Playing with classmates and siblings,
Praying for others and beloved ones
Lending hands for poor and needy
Watering the plants and feeding the hungry
Gives us a feel like a colorful rainbow.

10. HEALTH IS WEALTH

Life is a pleasant journey, not a race,
Maintaining good health is necessary and it's the base.
Eat leafy vegetables and fresh fruits to get strength,
Avoid unnecessary junk foods which are harmful to health.

Harmony of body, mind and spirit is called 'healthy',
Eat lightly, breathe deeply and live gently.
Give importance to quality of food than quantity,
Exercise regularly as it promotes your daily activity.

'Early to bed, early to rise' is a practice for well-being,
Wear mask and wash your hands as a good humanbeing.
Sleep well, when your body needs rest,
Laughter is the best medicine to exist.

11. INDIAN CULTURE

The sun is shining bright
My aunt came home by flight.
I welcomed her saying 'Namaste'
She blessed and kissed me with delight.
Oh! What a surprise, my mom said.
She brought her hot drinks and snacks.
They chatted about some family matter
Then she was served on a 'banana leaf platter'.
As the sun goes down
We went to the nearby town.
Astonished to see the Big temple's Shivratri mela
Which reflects the beauty of Raja Raja Chola.
'Folk dance 'and' Bharatanatyam' were performed well.
Everyone was surprised to see their skill
Be proud to be a citizen of this great tradition and culture.
Oh! Great leaders give importance to 'Agriculture'.

12. REAL BEAUTY

Oh! Beauty dwells in heart
A lovely face with a beautiful heart is so smart.
Service to humanity is service to God
Family and friends are the persons we have to guard.

Unexpected help to others is mercy.
Voluntary succor to others is charity.
Experiencing others' feelings is empathy.
Understanding someone's suffering is sympathy.

Affectionate person calls you, oh! Sweet heart,
Selfless person calls you, hey!soft heart
Good and gentle person says, Ah!kind heart
Honest and generous says,ha!open heart
Bless you!one who reads the poem has a cute heart.

13. STILL ANGRY WITH ME? JUST FORGET OR FORGIVE DEAR

I was too young and the season was spring
My dad gave me a box of sweets to share,
Selfishly, I ate some and hide some giving none
Still angry with me, forget it or forgive dear siblings.

It was a hot summer
My grandma asked me to bring some water,
Disobediently, I went with my friends for a dinner
Still angry with me, forget it or forgive dear grandma.

It was a chill rainy morning
My friend fell down, while cycling
Inhumanely, I walked without any worry
Still angry with me, forget it or forgive my dear friend.

First to forgive is the strongest,
First to forget is the happiest.

14. GOD

God is Love, Love is God
Unconditional love is the greatest gift, every creature fond.
Parents and teachers teach us the values of relationship bond,
Where there is love, there is God.

Truth is beauty, beauty is truth
Grow, mature and enjoy life being truthful.
It's the one way path to be fruitful
Where there is truth, there is God.

Inhumanity is not a virtue, virtue is humanity
Showing compassion and justice is a morality,
Respect all with dignity, kindness, humility,
Where there is humanity, there is God.

15. WHEN THE NATURE SPEAKS

Lovely woods are filled with frost,
The sun rises with a gleaming sight.
Birds come out from the nest with twitter and flutter,
Sheep and cattle get out of the shutter.

Trees breathe out oxygen for free of cost,
Oceans and seas give us salt to taste.
Mountains and valleys make us to cheer,
Plains and desert teach us not to fear.

Save rainwater to increase groundwater,
Discourage deforestation and encourage afforestation
Avoid pollution and try to find a solution,
Walk up with nature to understand its gesture.

Let nature be your teacher,
Worship and protect it for a great future.

16. IF WATER DIDN'T EXIST

Rain! Magical shower form cloud

Dry and dead become alive with proud

Top over the mountains or the valleys low

Flow as a river with endless glow.

Water is divine!

Living beings need water for their life time.

Water your plants every night

Next day you will see the lovely sight.

Water is a boon!

Realize and save the groundwater soon

Snow covers the polar region like blanket,

it's everyones duty to save water,save this planet.

17. I WILL NOT GIVE UP

Motivation is the key for many creations.

Determination strengthens you in difficult situations.

Optimism leads to great achievement.

Speaking truth guides you on the right pavement.

Goals motivate us and inspire us.

Challenges draw out the best in us.

Every day is a new day to learn and grow.

And then the whole world will be ours bro.

Do what you say

Say what you do.

Oh! My dear child, Don't give up

Trust in God, your life will spring up.

18. IN THE YEAR 2050

I wish '2050' will be a prosperous year,

Advancement of science and technology breaks many barriers.

People will lead a content and comfortable life,

But lack of food and water supply may lead to strife.

Global populatión is projectéd to rise,

Robots help people in many aspects of their lives.

Education and life style seems to imitate sci-fi,

Banking, shoppíng, business can be done so hi-fi.

New things will be invented by scientist,

It helps modern people wherever they like to exist.

Language barrier is altered by translation technology,

For a better life, let's follow 3R's as they're goals of ecology.

19. MY MOTHER

My mother is an angel on the earth
She protects and takes care of me from birth.
She sacrifices all the pleasures for my mirth,
Her guidance and counsel made me live worth.
When I was a baby, she sang lullaby,
She nourished me with a good education to qualify.
She helped me during tough times to modify,
A divine soul, all the living beings should glorify.
To preserve the human race is every mother's responsibility,
Her position is unique for the progress of the society.
Great men must respect her with equality,
Oh! Sweet mother, Hats off to your nobility.

20. FRIENDSHIP

Friendship is an essential aspect of relationship,
Loyalty and equality are the foundation of this 'unbreakable ship',
Caring and sharing makes a stronger bond,
Mutual respect is an ethic that everyone fond.
A true companion who is always genuine,
Devastates discrimination as their souls are like holy shrine.
Comforts like a mother in painful frustration,
Supports like a father in a critical situation.
Choose good friends with utmost care
Be sure, you will become a 'super star'.

21. REMINISCENCE

My childhood memories are like golden treasure,
Parents and teachers' affection has no measure.
Lived in a rural along with the nature,
Gardening was a hobby which gave me pleasure.
I played hide and seek with my peer,
Chased butterfly and dragonfly for cheer.
Chirping of birds were pleasant to hear,
Neighbours shared joys and sorrows as they're dear.
I was filled with joy and confidence to learn cycling,
Family and friends motivated concerning.
I spent the valuable time for study,
Blessed to be a good teacher is deserving.

22. MONEY IS IMPORTANT, BUT

Honey is good for health
Money is important for wealth.
Little drops of water makes mighty ocean
Help poor and needy with devotion.
Pearls can't replace patience
Diamond like character is an essence.
Education is better than emerald
Good morals are cuter than red coral.
Money can buy worldly pleasures
But sacrifice and sponsorship are heavenly treasures
Searching for money is a great quest
Sharing and spending for others is a real fest.

23. ONE WAY TICKET TO MOON

Neil Armstrong was the first man to walk on the moon.

Now I too get a chance to meet you soon.

Who said that? Only a billionaire can fly to the moon.

Even a poet of imagination can try with tune.

A powerful rocket is needed

The space flight lifted off and speeded.

It takes two days to reach

Wow! I uttered a joyful screech.

Moon's gravity is one-sixth of the earth

I felt stepping on moon is rebirth.

One way ticket to moon may be a dream world

Going back to earth ought to be the living world.

24. DANCE - AN EXPRESSION WITHOUT WORDS

Dance is one among the sixty-four arts

Graceful movement of body parts,

Especially to rhythm and music

Express one's emotions, ideas and tunic.

It's a wonderful therapy

Which helps to overcome sorrow and adversity.

Gives relaxation and makes a person to enjoy,

Enhance fitness and break the monotony.

"Bharatanatyam' the classical dance of South India,

Became famous for the expression called 'navarasa'.

The greatest entertainer 'Michael Jackson', the King of pop

Became popular by dance moves called moonwalk.

Dance is not only an art,

It's a way to get feelings out, a lovely sport.

25. LOVE & HATE

Love is always a sense of caring,
Mutual understanding between two souls and sharing.
Adorable experience to feel heaven on earth,
True exchange of ideas and thoughts are trustworth.
Love means to forgive those who are dear,
It's a feeling not only to cheer
But also to wipe their tears.
Divine source which cures all the ailments,
Natural tonic that boosts the immune of patients.
Darkness is destroyed by faintest light,
Hateness can be changed by affectionate sight.
Love is like oxygen, utmost need to survive,
Spread the fragrance of love and prove that you are alive.

26. FORGIVENESS, THY NAME IS WOMEN

Women are the backbone of a nation

But they suffer a lot due to gender discrimination,

They're responsible to build a good family,

But some people treat them shabbily.

Some women are betrayed by their spouse,

Many are slighted by their mother-in-laws,

Few are insulted by their co-workers,

Faces a variety of problems but the divine heart 'Forgives'.

Forgiveness is a blessing to the giver and the taker

Women choose the sweetest revenge, as they're, wiser,

Their hearts aré pure, restore peace as in heaven

Hence Forgiveness, thy name is women.

27. HAPPY LABOUR'S DAY

Labour's day is on 1st May,

Earlier, they worked 15 hours a day.

With unity they protested in a right way,

Hurrah! Now workers work 8 hours with proper pay.

It's a great day to honour workers in the nation.

Some people work 'overtime' without recreation

For the better life of their generation

Obviously, it's a glorious day of celebration.

28. MY SUPER MOM, MY LOVE

My super mom, my love

Makes home peaceful as a dove.

Great admin, who takes care of the family,

Plays multiple roles and she's a one man army.

Her contribution and sacrifices are immeasurable,

Unconditional love fills up every day pleasurable

She smiles though suffers a lot of pain.

Sacred beings who always work for our gain.

She wakes up early in the morning,

Completes all the chores at home with charming

She's an emergency doctor 24/7

Cures illnéss through hóme remedies.

May second Sunday is a special day

In India it is celebrated as Mothèr's day.

Dear mom, no one can compensate your sense of caring

May you live long with overflowing blessing.

29. EDUCATION

Education is a process of acquiring knowledge,
Empowers us to face challenges and to manage,
It makes a person to learn many skills,
Helps to suppress the social evils.
Education strengthens thé society,
It improves one's mental capacity and personality.
Leads to the discovery of multi innovation in medicine and technology,
An essential tool to eliminate unemployment and poverty.
The right to education act insists compulsory education
It aids the students to make better decision,
It plays a significant role in moulding culture and ethics,
Ultimately, Education is the doorway to sucess.

30. I HEARD A BIRD

One blessed morning, I woke up
As it was the time for day break,
I heard a pleasant 'cooing' sound of a cuckoo
It was so Sweet as a honey dew.
Shared the experience with my best friend,
He suggested that visit 'Vedanthangal' during the weekend.
Birds were migrated in huge flocks
Foreign birds feed their young ones on the bark.
When a flock is asleep
One bird will remain awake
Airplane wings are modeled after bird's wing,
We were mesmerized to see huge birds flapping.

31. LIKE A FISH HOOK

Tongues of some people are like fish hook
They speak só sweet like honey.
Makes it to believe and behaves so funny
Finally, they cheat our valuable time and money.
Appearances of some people are like fish hook
They look só gentle, sentimental with innocent faces,
Pretend to be a well-wisher and act like Nepenthes
In the climax, they trap and swallow our lives.

32. IF MY FOOTWEAR COULD SPEAK

If my foot wear speaks
It would say "Step forward"
My dear, go ahead without fear.
I'll accompany you, wherever you walk
In the utter darkness or in brightness,
In filthy place or in palace filled with fragrance,
I comfort your sole with a cozy feel.
Without me, it's difficult to protect your heel.
Barefoot is a symbol of poverty
I enhance your style and status in society.
Officials like prosecutors and judges worn for their dignity,
Everyone takes care of me with responsibility.

33. WHO IS RICHER?

Vision makes a greater person
Hopes and dreams lead to the new horizon,
Today is a good day to launch our goals
Knowledge and wisdom awaken one's soul.
Plan to achieve from past experience
Face challenges, nothing is mysterious,
Avoid overspending for the worldly pleasure.
Help out the needy, don't be a miser.
Be innocent as à child to be richer
Those who trust in the God are the richest.
Avoid debt and live within the limit
With a rich heart lift others to reach the summit.

34. WHEN I CLOSE MY EYES

When I close my eyes,

Cherished in the flood of my childhood memories,

I played with my friends like shimmering butterflies.

We made some dolls and models using potter's clay.

During rainy days, together we counted the colours of rainbows,

So, we were free from unpleasantness and stress.

When I close my eyes

My soul awakens, I meditate to self-evaluate.

As powerful moments are experienced in silence,

It's time to confess wrong deeds and mistakes

I thank God for all the showers of blessings.

As he protects, guides and gives us the perfect life.

35. I DON'T ALLOW MYSELF TO

I don't allow myself
To speak ill of others,
Because words are like sword
And it express our thoughts and intentions
if someone speaks ill don't bother.
I don't allow myself to believe gossips,
Because that destroys healthy relationship
And it leads to family and social problems.
If someone gossips their attitude is cheap.
I don't allow myself to be jealous on others
Because,it destructs our positive thoughts and emotion
And it brings uncertainty and rejection of us
If someone is jealous, inspire them to be zealous.

36. THE WAY I TOOK WAS DIFFERENT

Life is compared to an enchanting flower,

It blooms, spreads fragrance and the next day withers.

All living beings are protected by the supreme power,

With his guidance, I chose the right path in this sphere.

The way I took was different

It's an honest way, which raised my self- confidence.

I encountered some storms and difficult situation,

But, I hold truth and faith as my guide to come out of the frustration.

37. THE DAY YOU LEFT ME

The day you left me
It's like a new moon day.
I felt darkness everywhere
My eyes were filled with tear
As my little heart couldn't bear.
Alas! My grandmother passed away,
No one can replace your place,
You greeted and treated me with much grace.
My soul refused to accept the loss.
All the family members wept bitterly,
Since you guided and loved all sincerely,
Thank you for the values and valuables
Those golden moments will never come again.

38. WEEKEND

Weekend is meant for leisure,
Our family planned to go to 'Munnar' for pleasure,
Reached the destination and delighted in nature
Thrilled to see the passing clouds much closer.
We had a great day for the renewal of the mind,
Surrounded by rolling hills dotted with plants of many kind,
Excited to see 'Neelakurinji' which blooms once in twelve year
Decorated with herbal plants and free flowing river.
Enchanted to see the animal 'Varayadu'
It is the state animal of Tamilnadu.
India's best tea growing region made us to stun,
Return to the hometown as many works to be done.

39. I SALUTE

I salute the soldiers in the army
As they ensure national security and unity,
Vigils on the borders, ready to face dangers
Bravo, stands heroically before his enemies.
I salute the farmers all over the world
Farmers play a major role in our society.
Agriculture can reduce poverty
It raises the status of farmers and improves food security.
I salute the doctors as they care and cure
They protect the health of patients with comfort,
Doctors are responsible for improved life expectancy,
Living God, saves lives and creates a feel of ecstasy.

40. FATHER'S SHADOW IS ENOUGH

Father is more than
A hundred school masters,
Provide a sense of security
To his sons and daughters.
He taught me right and wrong
When I was too young,
Provides physical and emotional comfort,
To improve my education, he took immense effort.
He presented me a bicycle, in teen
Nurtured me to be self-disciplined to live as a queen,
With great reverence, I follow his footsteps
As my father is a real hero and God's gift.

41. CHECKMATE

Chess is a wise game
Played on a board of 64 squares,
With black and white colors
Competition between two players.
With plenty of cheer
King and Queen are lovely pair,
Two rooks, knights and bishops take care
Eight pawns step first to conquer.
Object of the game is to dare
And checkmate the opponent king without fear
Mind blowing game to improve concentration power
I dedicate this to Anand, Indian 'Grand Master'.

42. DEAR BACK BITERS

Backbiting is considered to be the greatest sin,
It hurts others a lot, don't do it for fun,
An evil act, slander someone in their absence,
Dare to discuss the matter in their presence.
A wise person thinks twice before he speaks,
It's a good attitude to avoid some mess.
Don't tell a person's mistake to another person,
As it tarnishes one's image and brings down his reputation.
Backbiting causes grudges, jealousy and corruption,
Dear backbiters, kindly stop it and respect fellow beings emotions.

43. DEAR GOPI JI, WE MISS YOU

Dear Gopi ji, We miss you a lot
You're a great person blessed with merciful heart
Especially, encouraged the younger generation
How can a beloved person digest your separation?
You looked majestic in the Student police cadet uniform
For the welfare of the students you laid a great platform.
A good role model, dedicated teacher and a nice gentleman,
You are still alive in our hearts as an adorable true man.

44. LETTER TO MY DEPARTED SOUL

My dear father-in-law,
Led a blessed life without flaw.
You are a man of perfection,
Your life history is a great lesson.
Humble person treated everyone with respect,
Loyal to the family members, never betrayed.
We miss you a lot, feel much depressed,
My soul longs and weeps to hear your loud voice.
Why did you depart?
Every day you fed the street dogs and crows,
A superhuman, inspired by the family.
Proud to be your daughter-in-law, as you're a charitable person,
Hope your divine soul rests in heaven.

45. AN ELEGY TO KI. RA

Mother Tamil has lost one of her identities,

On 17 May 2021, Ki-Ra passed away, an eminent folklorist.

A well-known short story writer and a novelist,

'Oruththi' film based on the short story 'Kidai' was a super-duper hit.

The legend was a Professor at Pondicherry University,

He was also a member of communist party.

A board member and a winner of 'Sahitya Academy'.

Though departed, still alive through his story.

A pioneer in writing stories in dialects,

Authored a dictionary called "Karisal Kattu Sollagarathy"

His works captured the lives of the 'Karisal Bhoomi'.

Alas! "We have lost the best story writer", regretted by our Chief Minister.

46. TIME MANAGEMENT

Manage your time
To attain new goals and shine,
It helps to improve your skill,
To be followed for being well.

Manage time to decrease anxiety,
Avoid heart disease and obesity.
Prioritise task and complete all with dedication,
And improve your professional reputation.

Manage the time as money effectively
Be like a bee and work more efficiently,
Good timé managemént makes a person greater
It's an irreplaceable asset to become smarter.

47. SOLITUDE

Solitude, a state of holiness for a sage,
It's not loneliness, don't feel like a bird in a cage.
A great moment of pleasure for a genius,
Experience the combination of quietness and convenience.
Freedom is considered to be great benefit of solitude,
Creativity can be sparked, to develop a great attitude.
Helps to discover self-identity, whenever confused,
Let's think over the architect of our lives to express gratitude.

48. RAMZAN, A FESTIVAL OF CHARITY

'Ramadan' is also known as Ramzan
Muslims begin their fast when sunlight touches the horizon.
It's the ninth month of Islamic lunar calendar
A special month, which brings blessings upon the believer.
Faith, prayer and Hajj gives them inner peace
Fasting improves their well-being ànd spiritual excellence
Zakat or charity is not only beneficial for the receiver,
But also a great reward for the giver.

Ramzan is month of great blessings,
Allah sent the first verses of the Quran to Mohammad.
It's a holy month as they're busy in prayer,
Learn self-control, patience and refuse all the pleasures.
A sense of generosity colors the festival,
As it's the time for charity, they sacrifice an animal.
They offer one-third for the needy
One-third for themselves, another for friends and family.

A golden opportunity for Muslims to support and share
Let's wish them 'Happy Ramadan' with cheer.

49. HAPPY BIRTHDAY CREATIVE WRITERS

Congrats to all Creative Writers.
We have completed one year in literary genre
Our admin gives us a topic to be penned,
Through writing and chatting, all become good friends.

New ideas and thoughts are shared
Many selfless hearts reviewed, guided and encouraged us,
Learnt so many good values through beautiful verses
On this great day, I pray to God to bless all of us.

50. MONKEY

Monkeys are tree dwelling,
Ancestors of human being
Notorious and social animals
Take care of babies as they're mammals.
Children are fond of watching
When it jumps and swings.
Different kinds are seen in zoos
They eat meat, fruits and leaves.
Chimpanzees are the most sensitive species
In Japan, monkeys are trained as waiters.
Lives in groups, groups are called troops
One and only animal to peel and eat bananas.

51. LIFE IS LIKE A....

Life is like a mirror

Always reflects the reality

Sometimes it's so hard to live

Bear the pain, as it makes a person strong.

It's a blessing of the Lord

Visualize your achievements,

Work hard to reach the goal

It's better to stay away from negativity.

Being alive is a celebration

Experience shapes a person's life

Do what your hèart and mind says

To maintain a healthy and balanced life.

52. WRITING HELPED ME WHEN

Writing helped me when
I havé been under lot of stress,
To write down my thoughts everyday
I maintain a diary with great interest.
An easy way to express my ideas
It helps to gain control of my emotions,
A great channel to express my situations
Of course, an efficient way to resolve my problems.
Writing creates an opportunity for positivity
Tracking the day to day important activity
Like medicine, it heals traumas and life threatening diseases
Also promotes my well-being and héalthy mental condition.

53. OUR NATIONAL BIRD

Our national bird is Peacock

Caged birds long for freedom, kindly unlock.

Colorful bird in iridescent blue and green plumage is so scenic,

Do not compare your life with others and be unique

When peacock fans its tail, looks so beautiful

Render service to the society and be dutiful.

Peacock, a sacred bird is a symbol of proud,

Tail feathers has' eye' markings of blue,red and gold.

The largest flying bird fascinates the human

Protect and care for the birds ánd be a superhuman.

54. LEFT ALONE IN A LONELY PLACE

When I was left alone in a lonely place
My mind raised a question in a husky voice,
Is this just to leave a person in an unknown land?
I searched everywhere, but none was there.
The sun set and the birds hurried into their nest
My heart was filled with horror and distress
My co-travellers and friends forget me, whom I trust
Luckily, the full moon raised a ray of hope like a mistress.
That night I bitterly wept and later slept,
Nature protected me like it's guest.
Surprisingly, the next day well-wishers traced me with great effort
I reached my residence with their timely help and support.

55. ONE DAY I WILL

One day I will be a 'Feminist writer'
Like the waves on the seas,
I'll create awareness through verses,
To fight against the domestic violences and crimes against women.
Let's wake up and lock up the evils like betrayal and cheating.
Women compete men in all spheres of life,
They do multiple roles, not merely a wife.
In the olden days women are mostly dependent
Now-a-days, education helps her to be independent.

Gender bias is the greatest barrier for the empowerment of women,
The word 'Women' itself says they're equal to men.
She contributes to natíon by joining social service and army,
Like a guiding stár, women work for the glory of their family.

56. FORGOTTEN HEROES

'Thanthai periyar' was an Indian social activist,
A politician who started a movement called self-respect.
Also known as father of Dravidian movement,
Rebelled against gender and inequality with great effort.
Raja Ram Mohan Roy was a great social reformer,
He was given a title 'Raja' by a Mughal emperor
He believed education to be an implement for social reform,
Took immense effort to abolish the evil practice 'Sati'.
Many freedom fighters sacrificed their life to 'Free' India,
But social reformers held the key to fight against 'evils'
They are the honorable forgotten heroes'.
I salute their hard work as they wiped people's sorrows.

57. MELODY

The Lullaby sung by mother,
Babble of the baby,
Twitters of the birds,
Burble of the waterfalls,
Pitter patter of the rain,
Clapping of audience,
Buzzing sound of a bee,
Gushing sound of the water,
Eolian sound produced by the wind,
Are all nature's melody
Which makes our lives lovely and lively.

58. GRIEF DISAPPEARS WHEN

Grief disappears when we accept,

In this world, Nothing is permanent.

Like sunny day and dark night

Grief and Joy are life's equal part.

Grief disappears when we have satisfaction,

With what we have and to think of the downtrodden

Because, if we do good, we'll feel good

As the Bible says "There is more happiness in giving than receiving".

Grief disappears when we listen to music

As it's an easy way to forget tragedies

We must accept the truth and fact,

Grief is like a new moon and joy is like a full moon.

59. A PEACEFUL SLUMBER

A peaceful slumber during night
Is an inevitable aspect for most of the living beings.
Good sleep for 6 to 8 Hours a day is incredibly vital for a human being.
So, it's better to avoid scrolling your mobile phone during late night.
Three things a person needs to inculcate and follow
A good diet, an exercise routine and a good night sleep.
To sleep on time and to wake up on time improves one's livelihood,
And also prevents any mental or physical blockages and hindrances.
Good sleep puts a person in good mood,
Otherwise it leads to depression, that's why some behave rude.
Sleep well to experience impressive health benefits,
To think better and have a better memory.

60. WHEN I LOOK BACK NOW, I REALIZE

When I look back now, I realize

And enquired myself "Why have I wasted precious minutes?"

In useless talks and in unwanted chores.

It hurts mé a lot and finding á better way to compensate.

We are highly responsible for what we are now

Our past actions determined our present

Our present actions determines our future

Being good to ourselves and to the world is the right choice.

When I look back now, I realize

Any situation can be favorable or unfavorable

But,it depends on how we react and handłe it,

Life is in our palm and choice is ours.

61. LEARN TO SAY NO

Like a leaf on the wind
We are pushed and pulled,
To say 'yes' to convince others
But, be honest to say No, no need to pretend.
Oh, my dear brothers and sisters,
Let's say no to cruelty,
Say no to untouchability,
Say no to domestic violence.
I think it's better to say 'No'
Because saying 'yes' to everyone
Increase the enmity and devastate our peace and joy
Learn to say 'No',to maintain a good relationship and to glow.

62. AN EMPTY NEST

Once I saw a Bay weaver's nest
A Beautiful abode for the bird to rest.
It was woven on a palm tree corner,
In order to escape from enemies and danger.
An engineer is hidden in a bay weaver,
Because it chooses a half grass and coir
To build its own nest with two chambers
One for its babies and another for its cute partner.
One day I noticed the nest on the ground,
Filled with surprise, I took in my hands but nothing found,
The bird might flew to new location and hence the nest abandoned
Learned about the well-disciplined life of the bird that astounded me.

63. MY DEBUT AS A WRITER

Writing is an excellent art to convey my thoughts
An easy way to express even sensitive facts,
A creative art which makes a person perfect
Of course one can feel positive vibes and great impact.

My debut as a Writer will be a blissful day
Awaiting for the occasion as a baby's first birthday,
A moment to express my gratitude to all who encouraged me
And a glorious event to thank God for guiding and moulding me.

64. MY DAD, MY HERO

My dad, my hero
Without him, I am zero.
With his guidance and support
I achieved some goals with little effort.

My dad is my fort
Only person who thinks of children's comfort,
He taught me good manners and ethics in life
Still he is guiding me to face all the strife.

My dad is a teetotaler
Who respects my mom as an equal partner.
An inspiration for mé to be perfect
I feel so proud to be your daughter, you deserve all respect
Long live with good health and happiness.

65. THE BEST IN ME

'Optimism' even in the difficult situation
I try to overcome the problem without hesitation
Showing compassion and kindness to fellow beings
Bless me to feel 'The world' a happier place.

As a teacher, I inculcate good social skills
Leadership qualities and civic responsibilities for my students.
I believe self-discipline is a great virtue
Like a shadow, good spirits follow us until the kingdom comes.

Meditation for a while, beaming a smile,
Honor the person who helped me when I was in a tight corner,
I never cheat a person who trust in me
I think these are the best in me.

66. SAVE ME TO SAVE YOU

Oh! my dear children,
Harvest rainwater,
To increase groundwater.
'Use dustbin' Don't scatter the papers.

Oh! my home makers,
Choose your hobby as a gardener
And invest your leisure to reduce pressure
Eat organic fruits and vegetables to stay healthier.

Oh! my masters,
Mother earth's lovely sons and daughters
To avoid pollution,flood and disaster,
"Go Green" and plant trees hereafter.

67. DEAR BODY, I LOVE YOU BECAUSE

Human body, a wonderful machine
Performs several functions,
Works well together in harmony
Without stopping for a second,
Hence, it's a valuable weapon.

Eyes helps me to see with glee,
Nose helps to breathe and sense the smell,
Ears play a crucial role to hear,
Flexible tongue responds with cheer,
And the skin provides a protective barrier.

Every college is controlled by a Dean,
Likewise, our vital organs are controlled by the brain.
Dear body, I love you because,
You're a lovely partner who responds my command,
And more precious than gold or diamond.

68. LIFE IS NOT A BED OF ROSES

Life is not bed of roses
Be brave to come across many challenges
In this voyage we face gentle breeze and furious storms,
But it's sure that we can feel calm after the storm,

Sometimes we are lucky to get, what we expect,
If you're not lucky, don't worry, just accept.
Remember, the night is darkest before dawn,
A colorful butterfly can be seen when it overcomes the pain.

Life is not just about existence
It's a journey to move on like a river
If the water gets stagnated, will it be pure?
Trust in yourself and succeed with persistence.

69. ISAIGNANI

Ilayaraja is a great Indian maestro,
He composed Thiruvasagam in symphony, the first Indian orator
A well-known music director and a play- back singer
An Inspiration to all as a lyricist and songwriter.

Proud to be a gold medalist in classical guitar
Orchestration for the film 'Annakili' made him a star
He invented a new Carnatic raga called 'Panchamukhi'.
Deserves to get the title 'Isaignani' by Kalaignar Karunanidhi.

His works are incomparable, a great genius,
Who composed soundtrack for more than thousand movies
His sheer talent and hard work won many awards and fans
I wish him all the success today and always.

70. IF YOU GIVE ME YOUR HEART

Heart is considered to be the token of love,
Love encompasses ever increasing positive energy.
Positive energy leads to determination
Determination ultimately helps to attain success.

Heart is the first organ to develop in fetus,
If any good things happen in our life
That's why we say emotionally "it touches my heart"
And it's a divine organ that functions nonstop.

If you give me your heart
I'll take çare of it like a precious earthen pot,
As it is so fragile, I will protect and care a lot,
I consider it the most valuable treasure till I depart.

71. SALUTE TO DOCTORS

Doctors are the living God in this planet,
They deserve great respect as they're life saviors.
Diagnose the patients with so much of patience,
Always try their best to recover the ailments.

MBBS programme is for five years
NEET is an entrance exam for the aspirants.
Every doctor takes the Hippocratic oath,
And they swear to follow ethics laid down for practice.

A doctor never asks class and caste, provide possible treatment
The great warriors are fighting against coronavirus,
With thermometers, stethoscope and ventilator as their weapons,
Hence, I salute the doctors for their heroic efforts.

72. 4 Re's

*(REDUCE, RECYCLE, RENEW, RECYCLE
GARBAGE)*

Eco-Friendly environment develops a nation,
It's our responsibility to avoid pollution,
We must follow 4Re's to maintain cleanliness
It's better to start from our home as it is next to Godliness.

It improves the quality of life and protects us from diseases,
Use natural products to ensure safety from all dangerous chemicals
Switching to energy-efficient appliances could reduce carbon emissions,
Avoid plastic and use reusable bags for groceries.
We have to take small steps to preserve our planet,
Enjoy the good things and rewards like a banquet.

73. SWEET SCHOOL DAYS, EMPTY CLASSROOMS

School days experience is like an invaluable treasure,
Where students from different environment gather with pleasures
It's a golden period to gain self-confidence and co-operation,
A holy place that encourages students to attain their ambition.

Morning assembly nurture the students for great future,
Thought for the day and teacher's motivation creates optimistic atmosphere
A holy place to be respected as it brings heaven on earth
Through sharing love, ideas and afternoon lunch brings mirth.

Unluckily, due to the pandemic and lockdown,
Classrooms are empty like a lonely desert
Students are attending online classes eating some favorite dessert
Parents and teachers hope, "Good times will come soon."

74. DREAM

Like a chocolate cream on a ice cake dreams makes us happy,
Though it is fake expert says "unfulfilled wishes comes as dream."
Sometimes we encounter horrible things,
That's why we scream.

One day I was in a thick forest
There was none with me to escort
The falls looks like a silver blade
I completely forget myself in the nature's delight.

Suddenly I heard the rustling sound,
Followed by a heavy down pour from rainy cloud.
I was drenched completely and shivering
Then I woke up with murmering realised,
Just a dream...

75. I CAN'T LIVE WITHOUT

My family helps me in maintaining stability,
Through love, respect and loyalty
It saves me from the anti-social elements in the society
Teaches me to be a responsible person and to improve my personality.
Teaching profession helps me to empower the students
And to boost their moral values and confidence
I teach them not only syllabus but exchanging good thoughts
Sharing ideas and guiding them in all ups and downs.
Hence, I can't live without my family and profession
As it made me realize the power of true love and self-respect.

76. MY HEALING MANTRA IS

Each and every person in this world is unique,
'Stay positive in thoughts and arise like a phoenix.
Everything happens for a reason,
Sow good to harvest the best.

My healing mantra is 'All for the best.'
Because the Almighty is watching us from womb to tomb.
He never do injustice to a good person
So I embraced silence and patience as my shield,
My obstacles passed like a passing cloud.

77. STRANGE HABITS

Good habits develop good manners,
To read and write are important skills for learners,
We should say 'sorry' and 'thank you' in desired occasions,
Respect others, irrespective of their age in all situations.

Being honest is good for everyone,
It's a good attitude, no need to fear anyone
We must be frank in our views and opinions
To lead a serene life and to avoid confusions.

Away from good habits are strange habits,
Sleep driving is a strange and risky habit
Some people eat wedge of brick and chunk of wood
We must avoid unnecessary and strange habits to be good.

78. IT IS BETTER TO BE ALONE THAN

It's better to be alone
Than to be in a crowd of foxes,
Foxes are deemed for cunning,
Likewise, some people's acting makes us stunning.

It's better to be alone
As it increase our selfconfidence,
To deal with adverse situations
And to save ourselves from distractions.

It's better to be alone
Instead of being overthrown,
And to avoid some moans and groans
Finally, to pray to God for the comfort zone.

79. DR. A.P.J. ABDUL KALAM

"Missile man of India"-Dr. APJ Abdul Kalam,
Lead a dignified life, deserves to get salaam
Though born in a poor family, never gave up education
Along with supporting the family, he completed graduation.

He was a member of the pokhran nuclear test,
Contributed a lot for the missles 'Agni and Prithvi without rest.
A man of simplicity and integrity,
11th President who had a vision to make India a great country.

An inspiration for the children who said "Dream, dream, dream,
Not during their sleep to scream
But while they're awake with a gleam
And to work hard with dedication to become supreme.

80. SWEET TREATS

Sunrise and sunset,
Blue sea and rainy clouds,
Waterfalls and snowfall,
Dewdrops and breezy wind,
Moonlight and twinkling stars,
Parrot's beak and baby's cheek,
Sea waves and cherry blossoms,
Unconditional love and peaceful dove,
Peacock's train and Himalayan shrine,
Are all nature's sweet treats.

81. IT'S IMPOSSIBLE

Oh! Cute little ants,
Though you're a small social insect
You can carry ten to forty times of your body weight
Worker ants maintain their nest.

Nest protects the čolony against their enemy,
We should learn from them, the great attitude harmony.
It's marvelous to see your power of adaptation,
Your way of organization shows determination.

I'm always eager to know what you communicate with each other,
Everyone is impressed by your sense of discipline
You teach us "Nothing is impossible."
Be active like an ant "Everything is possible."

82. CLOSE YOUR EYES AND SEE

Close your eyes and see
We can find a solution to reduce our stress naturally,
Confusion and tension says goodbye humbly
Mind becomes calm and we can think clearly.

Close your eyes and see
Memorable sweet moments make our cheeks to glow,
Sometimes shameful events give us a nice blow
But, it teaches us a lesson to be cautious to grow.

83. NOTHING IS STRANGE

Nothing is strange and permanent,
Every living being can survive, when adopted to the environment.
For a woman, Education is the most beautiful ornament,
Victory knocks the door of a person who works with involvement.

Life is like a tournament,
Confidence is the key to win and overcome impediment,
Marriage is a holy event and a sacred covenant
Bride and bridegroom should treat each other with respect.

84. THE CURE FOR MY PAIN IS IN

The cure for my pain is in 'humor'.
An invaluable sense that wipe out my tear;
One of the crucial quality for a teacher
To motivate the students, it's the need of the hour.

Being funny is the best way to get rid of depression,
Laughter is the only medicine, which gives relaxation,
And mákes our heart and mind as light as feather
That's why orators prefer humor for better performance.

Laughter and smile are universal signs to tell everything is fine.
Comedies are always better than horror movies.
As it improves one's memory and cardiovascular health
Those who have a sense of humor always shine like diamonds.

85. LIFE IS A GAME, PLAY IT

Life is a game, play it

Birth is a beautiful gift given by God to exist,

To lead our life in a good manner is an essential aspect,

It's our choice to choose good or evil before we exit.

Life is like mercury, handle with care

We should analyze the causes for rejections and failures.

Duty and relations are like the two sides of the same coin,

Everything happens for a reason, don't blame the circumstances.

Life isn't just about living independently,

Quality of life plays a huge importance in our society.

A person is valued based on career path and economic class,

So everyone should cherish and respect the 'precious Life.'

86. THE ART OF LEARNING

Learning is an art to achieve many new skills,
It makes a person's life so beautiful as daffodils,
Improves one's knowledge and it's a lifetime process,
Creative thinking and presence of mind leads to great success.
Discoveries and inventions can be done through learning,
Learning with good planning paves way for well-being.
The most valuable tool makes a person wiser through researching,
It improves curiosity and enthusiasm for better understanding.
Learning develops the skill of memorizing
Enhances the world of technology "keep on growing."
Strengthens one's character, mind and attitude,
Learning starts in the womb and it ends in the tomb.

87. KAMARAJAR, AN EYE OPENER

Kamarajar who was born in Virudhunagar
Deserves a unique honor as a chief minister,
One of the greatest leader acknowledged as the kingmaker,
An eye opener, responsible for bringing free education for the poor.

A disguised mother who introduced free mid day meal scheme,
To provide at least one meal per day was his noble aim.
Free school uniforms were given to poor students,
To weed out caste, creed and class distinctions.

Dams and irrigation canals were built for human consumption,
Steps were taken to improve the standard of education.
Like an engineer, he played a major role to develop Chennai's infrastructure,
An epitome of Tamil tradition and culture.

88. YOU CAME INTO MY LIFE

HOPE, you came into my life like a lighthouse
Darkness was driven out by your presence
Like a shadow, You follow me wherever I go,
Like a booster, you motivate me whenever I'm slow.

SELF CONFIDENCE, You came into my life like a clear crystal,
As you entered, fear and tear is replaced by cheer
'Believe in yourself' is a great verse that reduce my nervousness,
Those who are confident can lead their lives like princes and princesses.

ACTIVENESS, you came into my life like a busybee
Laziness faded away like the foam on the sea.
Honey bees are a good role model for precise compassionate community,
I try my best to be like a bee to create a harmonious society.

89. INDEPENDENT, YET IN CHAINS

Independent, yet in chains
Break the chain of dependence, through education
Break the chain of child labour for a healthy generation,
Break the chain of brutality to enhance glorious civilization,
Break the chain of poverty and raise the donation,
Break the chain of pessimism and be an inspiration,
Break the chain of food scarcity and encourage cultivation,
Break the chain of sorrows and believe every new day is for celebration,
Break the chain of illiteracy and guide the students by motivation,
Break the chain of domestic violence for the empowerment of women.
Let's unite and join hands together and succeed with co-operation.

90. DO SMALL THINGS WITH GREAT LOVE

Mother Terasa, the great women was born as a boon to orphans,
Dedicated her life to the dying and sick people in slums.
Like an angel she protected and gave life to destitute,
She'll be alive in the hearts of people till the earth exists.

She founded 'the missionaries of charity.'
A noble minded woman and a good role model for humanity.
Undoubtedly, a sainty lady with oodles of compassion,
She rendered her service with an ocean of patience and affection.

Despite being a non-Indian
She had spent her whole life helping Indian
She did even small things with great love, that's why she's pious,
She proved that God comes in the form of humans.

91. LONG LIVE DEAR BROTHER

Long live, dear brothers
I feel so proud to be your sister
Both of you are blessed to be an engineer and a doctor,
Politeness and kindness add beauty to your character.

When we were kids, occasional fights held for silly matters,
You are good in studies and responsibilities
Long live, my dear brothers
I pray to God to maintain a strong bond forever.

92. WHEN THERE WERE NO SMART PHONES

In the olden days, for more than thousands of years,
Verbal communication was the only choice,
When there were no smartphones
Secret messages were sent via pigeons.

Later drum beats and torches were used to communicate,
Soldiers leveraged smoke signals to warn the comrades.
Body language and tapping the rods were the signals for the prisoners,
Palanquins were used to carry letters.

Letter writing, the great art became a vital part to communicate,
Mass media like Radio, walkie talkie played an important role,
Now-a-days it's impossible to survive without instantaneous communication,
Let's use smartphones in a smart manner to accomplish our ambition.

93. I FEEL SAD BUT I DON'T KNOW WHY

I feel sad I don't know why
Like caged bird, sometimes I cry
It's because of stress due to pandemic
Spread of fungal infection makes the patients more pathetic.

I feel sad, when I see differently abled,
Obstacles and restrictions lead them to difficult situation
Some are physically challenged and some are mentally retarted
Helen Keller and Beethoven's life gives them a ray of hope.

I feel sad, when I hear about natural disasters,
Calamities like earthquake and floods have increased
Citizens must learn the basic ways to save themselves
And the government should take more responsive measures.

94. RED CROSS

Red cross was found by Henry dunant
"I owe to serve" is the motto of this movement
To help the stranger whom you don't know
For its through your kindness humanity is built.

Impartiality makes no discrimination
It breaks the barrier-class and race of a nation.
Neutrality gives the ray of hope and confidence
Confidence is the spritual power for strengthening peace.

Independence is freedom that comes from heart, mind and soul
It gives courage and determination to achieve many goals.
Voluntary service is what you provide your family and fellow beings
Such as Blood and eye donation is the need of the hour.

Unity and togetherness brings much more success
It creates an honest path and ability to explore new achievements.
Universality reminds us about equal status and responsibilities.
Its your debt to serve, share and help each other.

95. RISE UP LIKE THE PHOENIX

Rise up like the Mythical bird of Greek
Learn from the phoenix who are emotionally weak.
Heard it lived in the Arabían desert.
Fruits and spices are its only dessert.

Fabulous bird associated with immortality
Flaming peacock, a symbol of eternal city
Large as an eagle with golden plumage
It's a role model for human courage.

Brilliant scárlet bird survivé so many years
Ready to meet life 's end with cheer.
Immolate itself on the altar fire
Young phoenix rose from the ashes without any fear.

Flew, with the ashes to 'Heliopolis'
Complete the formalities liké people in 'metropolis'
Life of Christ tells us cross before salvation
Phoenix also reveals us 'hardships before gratification.'

96. MY SUCCESS LADDER

Books are my successful ladder,
Reading is an expensive hobby.
Read novels ånd fiction chapter by chapter,
It's a good companion for a traveler.

Skim and scan books for brain health,
One and only source for mental health
Read again and again to gain knowledge,
It's the prosperous way for students in college.

Encourage kids, with the reading hobbý,
It helps them to win so many trophies.
Improves memory and concentration,
Books are valuable friends, güide us to perfection.

97. WELCOME APRIL

With so much happiness in my sóul,
Welcome! April to achieve many goals.
O Lord, protect us like fortress and rock,
And bléss us to fly and sing like a lark.

Don't worry about the errors in the past,
Erase it, with the exploration of new things at present,
Extend warm greetings to your fellow beings and pets,
Trust, magical things will happen next.

As the pandemic is spreadíng everywhere,
Take cáre of your kids like a polar bear.
Try to avoid spreading rumor
It causes more destruction than tremor.

Even the most beaútiful rose has thorn,
From the filthy water only lotus is born.
Be yourself and grow up like a full moon
Let's pray for the corona patiénts to get well soon.

98. I WAS MOVED WHEN

Once, when I was a student
I was waiting in the platform for the arrival of train,
With some luggage's and school bags ,after vacation
I was returning back to the boarding school.

As soon as the train arrived
All rushed into the compartment like buzzing bees
I too hurried like a kite on the wind
To find a comfortable seat for me.

I reached my destination
Shocked and expressed,
Alas! I had lost one of my bags at the station,
Felt nervous, as I lost my record notebook.

I knelt down,prayed to God
Luckily, a good hearted person
Found the bag and handed over to the station master,
The station master informed my headmistress about the bag.
When I heard the news, I was really moved.

99. A LETTER FOR YOU

A letter to you-Dear God
You created the universe with a plan and a purpose,
Like Adam and Eve, we lost your grace because of wickedness
Sometimes through painful situations you teach us good lessons.

Everybody knows "God is good and just".
He allows some problems to perfect us.
Now-a-days, people are taking 'stressful rest.
'We plead your mercy and longing for the best.

100. LOCK DOWN

Lockdown 2020-2021
Followed by the people in remote village and city,
Patients could not get enough oxygen,
Everyone feels so pity.

Corona virus spreads from infected person
Through cough and sneeze,
To avoid the risk, don't shake hands, wear mask,
Stay home, stay safe please,
Meditate, eat healthy fruits and vegetables,
Talk to someone whom you trust,
Create awareness among people in the neighborhood,
Because prevention is the best.

Human civilization not only in India
But all over the world are facing threat for survival.
Now-a-days people have a great fear to attend
And pay respect to their loved ones funeral,
Dear friends pledge to maintain social distance
And lockdown orders given by the government.
To knock down covid-19.

About The Author

Mrs. R. Ezhilarasi, M.A., B.ED., M.phil.,BT Assistant
(English)GGHSS, Arakkonam.

Mrs. R. EZHILARASI M.A., B.ED., M.phil., has been working as a B.T. Assistant Teacher (English) at G.G.H.S.School, Arakkonam in Ranipet District. She has 22 years of teaching experience. She is a passionate reader and a writer. She has written more than two hundred poems. One of her poems was published in the Anthology "Glitters of Creative Writers" which was edited by Mrs. D. Brinda Srinivas. (English Teacher). She was awarded Seermigu Teacher's Award in the year 2010. She is the counsellor for Junior Red Cross movement in G.G.H.S.School Arakkonam. She always motivates her student to learn good morals and also to serve fellow beings. She is a lover of nature and has a passion for reading. She is a lover of music also. Some of the memory poems for std 6 to 10 were sung by her and uploaded in her you-tube channel "Learn and Shine with Ezhil". She is a sincere dedicated teacher.

Her dreams and desires are to impart knowledge and discipline of her lovable students. She feels so proud to be a little drop in the Mighty Ocean of Literary Genre.

www.ingramcontent.com/pod-product-compliance
Lightning Source LLC
Chambersburg PA
CBHW072046150726
47996CB00015B/1916